60

table of contents

Cardmaking for Scrapbookers

2

48

TAKE NOTE
of Life Events

Celebrate any noteworthy event in your life—and in the lives of your family and friends—with a card made just for the occasion.

Baby Boy Joy

A special photo of the new arrival adds a precious touch to a birth announcement. Or, to make a baby card congratulating the new parents, use a stock photo as designer Lori Bergmann did, *opposite*. To obtain stock photos, purchase a CD from one of several manufacturers or download separate images for free or a small fee off the Internet. Lori enhanced this stock image by hand-stitching along the border and along the edges of the fabric label.

Design by Lori Bergmann

baby's birth...wedding & anniversary...graduation...birthday...other occasions bundle of BOY

CUTE AS A BUTTON

Jennifer Ditz McGuire topped card stock with a pretty patterned paper and added text to a punched 2-inch-diameter circle, leaving space in the center for a button. She drew a smile and hair on the button and adhered the button to the circle. On the blue card, she attached the left half of the circle to one flap, and on the pink card, she attached the circle in the center of the top front. She finished the pink card with an eyelet in each corner.

Designs by Jennifer Ditz McGuire

Watercolor Wash

Diluted watercolor paint tints the small checked papers on the front of this card, *right,* so that they more closely match the colors of the other paper. After securing the strips of paper on the card front, Alison Beachem printed her text on a transparency and attached it with adhesive, hiding the seams with lengths of polka-dot ribbon.

Design by Alison Beachem

Baby Face

For a totally nontraditional birth announcement, Vivian Smith suggests thinking in circles. Her design, *left,* fits into a square $4\frac{1}{4}$-inch envelope and is sure to get noticed when it arrives in the mail. To make the announcement, she used a circle cutter to cut three 4-inch card stock circles. A trimmed photo fills one of the circles, and the announcement, printed on white vellum, fits on top. Other details appear on the layers beneath. An eyelet, punched through all three layers, is set loosely enough to let the circles spin open and reveal the details within. *Note:* Square envelopes require additional postage.

Design by Vivian Smith

Girlish Glitter

This sweet baby announcement, *left,* by Erin Terrell gets its shimmer from card stock squares covered in glitter and decorative buttons attached with ribbons. Erin then added extra dimension by mounting the squares with adhesive foam.

Design by Erin Terrell

ABC Announcement

With the front of this card, *below,* Shannon Smith's goal was to keep recipients guessing the baby's name a little longer. The cover of playful letter-pattern paper gives nothing away. Inside, she printed the announcement information, including the baby's name, of course, in a font and colors to match the exterior pattern paper. Two punched holes along the card's fold make room for a pretty organza ribbon.

Design by Shannon Smith

baby's birth

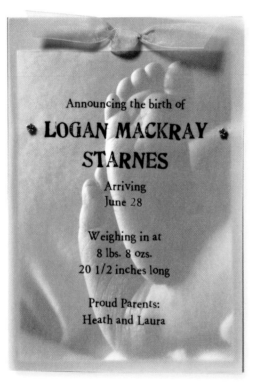

Announcing the birth of
LOGAN MACKRAY STARNES

Arriving
June 28

Weighing in at
8 lbs. 8 ozs.
20 1/2 inches long

Proud Parents:
Heath and Laura

Tiny Toes

A photo of a newborn's toes makes this announcement, *above,* a work of art as well as a memento. Nichol Magouirk had duplicate prints of the photographs made and mounted each on light blue card stock, leaving a wider border at the top for a bow. She printed the announcement on white vellum and secured the vellum to the card with ribbon threaded through holes punched in the top margin. Adding small embellishments such as beads, buttons, eyelets, or stickers makes each announcement extra special.

Design by Nichol Magouirk

SLIDER STATEMENT

A slider-style announcement gives recipients just a peek at the good news inside! To make this slider, the *Scrapbooks etc.* staff used a pattern (see page 92) to assemble the sleeve and measured and aligned the "It's a girl!" text so it shows through the circles. A caution: Be sure to arrange the rest of the print information so it isn't visible through the holes. Attaching the instruction "Pull" to the end of the slider lets recipients know it's okay to slide the message out of the card.

Design by the Scrapbooks etc. *staff*

SILVER SPARKLES

Whimsical wedding wishes grace these playful cards by Jennifer Ditz McGuire. The "charms" card, *above right,* includes a practical gift of two wineglass charms stitched to the front. To make a sturdy backing, Jennifer matted the silver paper onto card stock and then stitched the charms onto the layers. The silver paper is matted onto layers of metallic-gray paper and a base of white card stock. The bride-and-groom card, *above left,* includes panels that open in the front like the double doors of a church. Jennifer covered the front with pieces of patterned paper cut to size and matted. Stickers adhered to one panel and a sparkly ribbon closure complete the card.

Designs by Jennifer Ditz McGuire

More than Candy Kisses

This card, *right,* proves a point: The simplest ideas often have the greatest impact. A row of tags from chocolate Kisses candies definitely gets Brenda Lesch's message across. Brenda adhered the tags to a layered card stock background, then added a heart sticker and tiny greeting to flank the Kisses tags. A machine-stitched chain of thread connects the graphic elements.

Design by Brenda Lesch

Silver Anniversary

All eyes are drawn to the silver metal tag on this anniversary greeting constructed by Julie Medeiros, *below.* Julie created the embellishment with a metal tag adorned with silver leaf and a splash of acrylic paint. She attached the tag with a gauzy ribbon and adhered it to one edge of the patterned paper on the card front.

Design by Julie Medeiros

Wedding Memento

Ivanka Lentle created this card, *above,* for her nephew, not only to represent the love between him and his bride but also as a keepsake. She accented the ivory card with a subtle soft green patterned paper and then layered on small rectangles of ivory script-patterned and textured papers. After removing the vellum from a square metal-rim tag, she strung two heart charms onto a narrow green ribbon and tied them to the frame with a bow. To give the title a muted look similar to the script-patterned paper, she first stamped the letters onto scrap paper and then stamped them onto ivory card stock without reinking. Before attaching the title, she cut the words into three strips and tore the bottom edges.

Design by Ivanka Lentle

Keep reaching for the stars!

Congratulations,
Graduate!

graduation

SHINING STAR

Reaching for the stars is the theme of this graduation card by Susan Cobb. Susan cut a window in the front of the card to showcase a multifaceted star. To make the star, she cut two stars each from medium blue and light blue papers, matched the points with right sides facing out, and glued them together. To make the star dimensional, she cut slits in both stars about halfway from a point toward the center and then simply slid the two together. She hung the star in the opening with 32-gauge silver wire and attached a bow of silver thread to adorn the top.

Design by Susan Cobb

Congrats to the Grad

A metal-accented card, *above,* contains a surprise any grad will be thrilled to receive—cash! Erin Terrell folded a 7¼×11-inch sheet of card stock at 3¼ inches and again at 7 inches. Then she glued the sides of the lower flap, leaving the top open to slip money or a check inside. The metallic-look inset is a sheet of embossed crafting metal; Erin used a lettering template to spell out the message and finished the metal with star-shape nailheads.

Design by Erin Terrell

The Sky's the Limit

Graduates often toss their mortarboards into the air, so Laurel Albright gave her favorite graduate a flying start with one lifted by numerous "kites" in place of tassels, *right.* She chose appropriate school colors for the card.

After cutting out the cap, she cut gold metallic embroidery floss into different lengths. Then Laurel attached these to a layered card stock background. To make the cap center, she cut a 1-inch strip of quilling paper, rolled it into a tight circle, and glued it to the cap top. The kite-shape tassel ends are formed from cut quilling-paper strips and glued to the floss. A tassel glued to the roll on the top is the finishing touch. Patterns begin on page 92.

Design by Laurel Albright

Petite Presents

Sixteen tiny packages send sweet birthday greetings to a special 16-year-old. According to designer Jean Wilson, even if you can't cut a straight line, you'll be able to make this card, *right*. All of the squares are roughly cut, and the smaller boxes are made from snippets of patterned papers. A message on a thin strip adhered below the "packages" completes the sweet sentiment.

Design by Jean Wilson

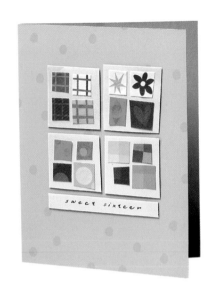

LONG ON WISHES

Premade embellishments simplified constructing this card for the *Scrapbooks etc.* staff. A long rectangular strip of card stock folded accordion-style forms five faces, which the staff defined with colored card stock. Cupcakes embellish three of the faces, a heartfelt message fills two of them, and a pretty ribbon ties everything together so it's ready for delivery.

Design by the Scrapbooks etc. *staff*

An Old-Fashioned Look

A little boy's silhouette—either hand-drawn for the occasion or vintage like this one, *left,* used by Kelly Rawlings—adds a sweet old-fashioned sentiment to a birthday greeting. Kelly adhered the silhouette to an inset paper and accented the card with buttons and a vintage ribbon.

Design by Kelly Rawlings

Party Punch

Punches do all the work on this simple card, *below.* Veronica Koh punched squares from pink and yellow card stock and adhered them to the front panel of a white card stock base. The hat, cupcake, balloon, package, and pink oval are punched shapes as well. She even used a hole punch to make the dots on the hat. She set eyelets in holes punched in each side of the pink oval and threaded them with ribbon as the final touch.

Design by Veronica Koh

A Bouquet for the Big Day

Embossing adds texture to this cheery birthday greeting, *above.* Nicole Gartland covered a rectangle of cream card stock with Ultra Thick Embossing Enamel, heated it, and adhered the vase and flowers to the embossed card stock. She stitched the flower stems with embroidery floss and matted the piece with green card stock. Alphabet stickers centered in silver conchos add another dimension; they're finished with a glossy coat of clear acrylic glaze.

Design by Nicole Gartland

How Old Are You?

Shannon Landen enhanced the birthday-candle theme of this card, *left,* by carefully burning away the bottom front of the card. The base of the card is made from pink and purple papers adhered back to back. She cut off the bottom portion of the card front and then used a lit match to burn the new bottom edge. (For safety's sake, Shannon recommends standing over a sink with the water running while you burn the edge.) She then adhered cutout candles to the inside of the card, attached tags with eyelets, and embellished the tags with letter stickers.

Design by Shannon Landen

Iced Cake

A nontraditional opening gives this card, *below,* a twist. Kathleen Paneitz started with a square of white card stock as a base; next she cut a window out of green paper, folded the top edge over the square, and glued the edge in place. Inside the window, Kathleen made the cake by running glue in the shape of the cake and pressing glitter into the wet glue. She added a card stock candle and a punched flame to the cake and then strips of vibrant card stock for a border. A ribbon strung through two eyelets set on each side of the card ties it closed.

Design by Kathleen Paneitz

Bright Birthday Greetings

Watercolors give this card, *above,* a happy-go-lucky visage. Donna Downey cut pieces of watercolor paper to fit the front of the card and painted each a different color using watercolor crayons. To blend the colors, she dragged a moist sea sponge across each one in a sweeping motion. The squares are simply mounted on the front of a white card; narrow satin ribbon covers the seams and gives the card the appearance of a wrapped gift. Donna printed her sentiment on a sheet of paper and inserted it into a metal-rim tag.

Design by Donna Downey

LOTS OF CANDLES

Card stock is the primary material Lindsay Ostrom used to make this eye-catching birthday card. Lindsay cut six rectangles from various colors of card stock and attached them to a sheet of white card stock. Then she mounted candle-shaped cutouts on foam squares to make them stand out. A reinforced ring tag tied with colorful string hangs from an eyelet set into the lower right corner. Lindsay used markers to write her message and to outline the elements.

Design by Lindsay Ostrom

BACK TO SCHOOL

Preprinted die cuts highlight this pair of colorful cards celebrating the return to school. For the apple card, *above right,* Erin Terrell adhered a die-cut frame to a folded piece of card stock, leaving the center cutout connected on one edge. The flap lifts up to reveal a photo of the featured child.

To make the die-cut card, *above left,* the *Scrapbooks etc.* staff combined small square die cuts and squares of solid card stock for a clean, simple look. The die cuts are mounted on adhesive foam for added dimension.

Designs by Erin Terrell and the Scrapbooks etc. *staff*

Applauding Success

Helen Naylor made this "success" card, *below,* using soft pastel tiles and squares of card stock to dress up the front. She mounted the tiles ridge side down so they look as though they're floating on the card. Her tips for affixing mosaic tiles to cards or layouts include: (1) Arrange the elements first, placing the tiles where you want them; (2) use a piece of card stock to gently scoot the tiles to their final position, keeping them in order as you move them; (3) one by one, put a bit of adhesive on the tiles and press them in place. Clear-drying liquid glue and adhesive dots work well. Allow the glue to dry for at least 20 minutes before moving the design.

Design by Helen Naylor

Enjoy the Trip

Tracy Kyle turned a vintage postcard found at an antiques store into a stunning bon-voyage card, *above.* She cut out the middle section of the postcard and mounted it on card stock, attaching it to the card front. Then she melted several layers of clear embossing powder over the image to give it a shiny look and, when cool, mounted it on the card face with adhesive foam.

Design by Tracy Kyle

Fringe Benefits

This versatile card, *right,* designed by Jennifer Ditz McGuire can be adapted to any occasion deserving of a congratulatory message—simply change the color scheme and inside message to fit the occasion. Jennifer started with white card stock and covered it with patterned paper. She adhered a section of beaded trim to fit the card front and used sticker letters to spell "congratulations" along the right edge.

Design by Jennifer Ditz McGuire

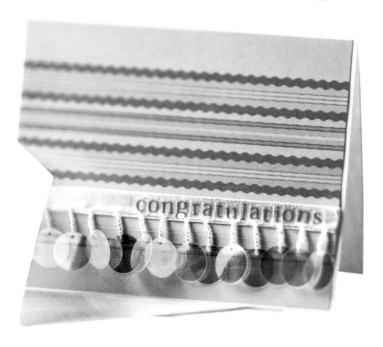

seasonal
greetings

Every season has its own reasons for celebrating. Mark these special dates by sending cards year-round.

CONFETTI TOSS

Erin Terrell used transparency film to make a pocket for confetti on this contemporary greeting card. The message is printed on the film using a color ink-jet printer; Erin added clear embossing powder before the ink dried. She used a template to cut the card shape from a sheet of white-backed patterned blue card stock and then lined the inside lower edge with a strip of colorful striped card stock.

Design by Erin Terrell

Gear Up for the New Year

This sophisticated greeting, *left,* by Faye Morrow Bell gleams with metal washers found at the hardware store and a stamped strip of crafting metal mounted along the card bottom. The clock face is stamped, and the clock's "gears" are metal lock washers. The metal message is attached to the card with mini brads.

Design by Faye Morrow Bell

Bright Star

This card, *below left,* shines with metallic printed papers. Susan Cobb used a template and a silver pen to trace the star window and then cut it out with a craft knife. Silver paper behind the window and behind the caption bring more sparkle to the card front. Tiny punched stars at the edges complete the caption box.

Design by Susan Cobb

A Vintage New Year

Vintage prints and silver accents give Erikia Ghumm's card, *right,* classic style. Her time-saving tip: Purchase a white card that already has windows in it. Erikia adhered vintage images to the back of the card front and embellished them with stickers and silver glitter. She punched two small holes 2 inches apart on the fold to add a gingham bow. To hide the piecework on the inside, she adhered a square cut from white card stock ⅟₆ inch smaller all around than the card front.

Design by Erikia Ghumm

winter

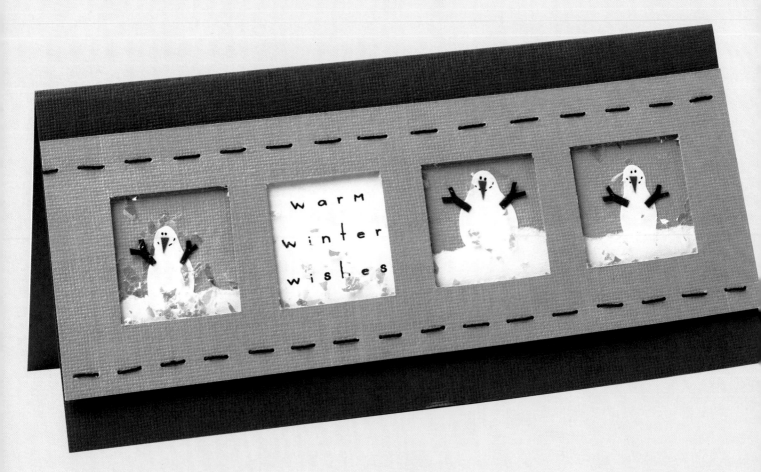

A TRIO OF WELL-WISHERS

This clever card by Helen Naylor is worth the effort. Helen punched four windows in the light blue card stock and covered them with an acetate strip, attaching the acetate with double-stick tape on the back. She placed narrow strips of adhesive foam around the window edges to form shaker boxes, hand-cut snow people and drifts for three of the boxes, attached the figures to squares of background paper, and printed her message to fit in the fourth box. Helen poured chunky glitter inside the well of each shaker box and carefully removed the backing paper from the adhesive foam, pressing the background images onto each square backing piece. To finish, she stitched along the top and bottom of the light blue card stock and adhered the piece to the backing card stock. Patterns begin on page 92.

Design by Helen Naylor

I Love Snowmen

To share her love of winter, Leslie Lightfoot designed this card, *above,* to express her feelings. Larger-than-life photo corners helped her make a statement. Leslie's tip: "Cutting a large slide-mount frame in half diagonally yields two oversize and distinctive photo corners that really highlight an image on a page. You can achieve an equally cool look with just about any type of frame—die cut, leather, or thin metal—that can be halved."

Design by Leslie Lightfoot

Snowman Lineup

Blue patterned paper makes a cool backdrop for a clan of snowmen on this card, *below,* by Helen Naylor. A pattern makes cutting the figures a snap; some of the snowmen are positioned behind the snow hill, and others stand in the forefront. Helen stitched on tan thread to create arms and attached an acrylic letter to each figure's middle to spell out her message. Patterns begin on page 92.

Design by Helen Naylor

Snow Shaker

A snow globe was Helen Naylor's obvious inspiration for her unique card celebrating the winter season, *above.* Helen started by assembling the inside of the globe, creating the snowman using a pattern and decorating the figure with buttons and a pen. The globe is made of two circles cut from a plastic sheet protector and one from white card stock. Ripping the white circle makes the snowy background inside the globe. She glued the "snow" to the back of the snowman and sandwiched the figure between the plastic circles. Using temporary adhesive to keep the pieces together, she stitched around the edges, leaving a small opening at the bottom. Then she added glitter flakes and closed the opening. The base is made of embossed crafting metal. Patterns begin on page 92.

Design by Helen Naylor

Frosty Charm

The recipient of this card, *below,* by Anita Matejka will be charmed by its simplicity and the delicate snowflake charm. Anita attached pale blue card stock to the card front by setting an eyelet in each corner and then adhered the metal charm to the card center. To finish, she printed "snow" on white vellum, tore the vellum and centered it on the card, and then stitched along each edge.

Design by Anita Matejka

Gentle Snowfall

To craft a wintry card, *above,* that would be as unique as the recipient, Karen Burniston chose a snowflake theme. She punched three snowflakes from card stock, rubbed them with a VersaMark ink pad, and heat-embossed them with several layers of clear embossing enamel. Dropping tiny silver microbeads into the last layer of embossing enamel adds a snowy sparkle, as does the scattering of snowflakes she punched from silver paper. The silver flakes are attached to the card with silver brads with blue rub-on centers. Mini eyelets hold the word "snowflakes" in place.

Design by Karen Burniston

Winter Warmth

Send warm-hearted thoughts to a friend or family member, as Helen Naylor did with this wintry-blue card, *left.* Helen cut mittens from a pattern and decorated the pair with hand-stitching and punched snowflakes. She chalked the edges of a strip of white card stock and stamped "Warm Hands" on it. To attach the wording strip to the card, she punched holes near each corner of the strip and threaded them with dark blue floss. Patterns begin on page 92.

Design by Helen Naylor

WINTER GREETINGS

This playful card is decorated with a flurry of snowflakes. Nichol Magouirk chose blue-stripe paper to cover the card stock base and stitched it to the base with white thread. She stamped a letter on each of six jewelry tags and rubbed the tag edges with silver ink and then stamped "warm" and "wishes" onto the card. Each jewelry tag is attached to the card front with a snowflake brad.

Design by Nichol Magouirk

spring

Happy Spring!

Flying Free

A trail of pastel eyelets leads to a fluttering butterfly on this card by Kathleen Paneitz, *above*. To make the butterfly, Kathleen embossed two butterflies onto yellow card stock and one onto vellum; she glued the vellum butterfly to a yellow butterfly, gluing only in the center so the wings would appear to flutter. Next, she cut the center from the remaining yellow butterfly and glued it to the center of the vellum butterfly. The antennae are made from gold wire that was coiled around an embossing stylus. Pastel eyelets form the butterfly trail.

Design by Kathleen Paneitz

PRETTY PASTELS

Gathered gracefully by a bow, these lovely layered pastel papers, *above*, chosen by Susan Cobb are a reminder of springtime colors and scents. Susan began with a piece of green paper to which she adhered a smaller rectangle of floral-pattern paper. She cut flaps from striped paper and attached them to the green paper, rounding the edges and tapering the green border. Ribbon threaded through slits in the flaps elegantly ties the card closed.

Design by Susan Cobb

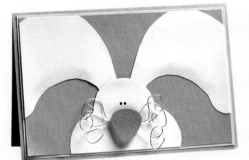

The Bunny Hop

A lovable, rascally rabbit noses his way onto the front of this Happy Easter card by Joanne Wesley, *left*. After cutting the head and ears from card stock, Joanne chalked the ears, rubbing the edges to soften them. She adhered the pieces onto contrasting card stock and then attached it to a folded piece of 8½x11-inch card stock so that the ears and head align with the edges of the folded card. The head is attached over the ears. To make whiskers, Joanne curled six 4-inch lengths of thin wire around a pencil, flattened the wire by hand, and used foam tape to attach them to the card. The bunny nose, also attached with foam tape, covers the area where the whiskers are attached. Patterns begin on page 92.

Design by Joanne Wesley

Time for Play

Spring is the time for outdoor fun, as Kathleen Paneitz demonstrates in this playful card, *above*. To make the pinwheel, she cut a square piece of card stock and cut it diagonally from each corner about halfway to the center. Then she folded the corners to the center and inserted a paper fastener to hold them in place. The stem is cut from wood-pattern paper.

Design by Kathleen Paneitz

Golden Greeting

The exquisite color work on this card, *right*, by Jan Achiu was created by tearing bits of paper and gluing them onto card stock to create multicolor, multitexture paper. She swished a glue stick over the collage, poured gold embossing powder over the papers, shook off the excess, and then melted the powder with a heating tool. Then she cut nine squares of the collage paper and punched the corners of four of them before attaching to the card front. A few extras—such as gold foil and a message stamped in gold—take this keepsake card from rags to riches.

Design by Jan Achiu

EDGED IN EYELET

The base of this lacy card is pink parchment and white vellum. Jean Wilson scalloped one edge with paper edgers and trimmed ⅛ inch from the opposite edge. To make the eyelet pattern, she aligned the edges and punched teardrops and large circles through both layers. To attach the ribbon, she punched two holes 1½ inches apart along the fold and threaded ribbon from the inside of the card and back through, leaving a small loop in each hole. She threaded a second piece of ribbon through the loops, leaving a tail at each end. Trimming the ribbon ends in a V shape and tightening the ribbons on the inside of the card are the finishing touches.

Design by Jean Wilson

Potted Greetings

For a twist on stickers, Jean Wilson backed hers with vellum to create colorful die cuts that show a flowerpot in bloom, *right*. To make the card, Jean adhered vellum-backed flower stickers to green florist's wire attached the wire to the card with pop dots. The message is printed on white card stock layered on border widths of other colors of card stock, with stickers substituting for the O's in the message. When adhering the message to the card, Jean allowed the square to extend beyond the fold.

Design by Jean Wilson

A Gift Inside

As a Mother's Day surprise, Leslie Lightfoot stitched coordinating papers to create a pocket that holds a spa gift certificate in her card, *below*. She decorated the card with a handful of pretty and petite embellishments, including a tiny photo to add personality. Zigzag stitching finishes the left edge.

Design by Leslie Lightfoot

A Jewel of a Card

Aiming for a soft, feminine touch, Kathleen Paneitz chose pretty pastel papers and cut a scalloped square to frame a punched daisy in the center of this card, *above*. She also punched small holes in the corners of the scalloped square and strung embroidery floss through them to highlight the frame. A flat-back jewel in the daisy's center finishes the card.

Design by Kathleen Paneitz

summer

SIZZLIN' SUMMER COLORS

Who says red and green are just for Christmas? Shannon Tidwell used shades of red and green to welcome summer on this eye-popping greeting. The paper Shannon started with featured blue and beige dots, which didn't match her scheme, so she covered the dots with punched red circles and green circle die cuts. A red wooden flower embellishment, a game piece for the second letter "M" in "summer," and red twill tape add texture to the contemporary card.

Design by Shannon Tidwell

Sharing Patriotism

Jean Wilson created this patriotic card, *below,* with patterned papers and a multifold card pattern. Jean cut the white background, blue insert, and white starburst from card stock, using the patterns. The postage stamps were cut from images on a sheet of patterned paper and matted. To finish the card, Jean cut a strip of paper for the front panel and hand-lettered the text. Patterns begin on page 92.

Design by Jean Wilson

Impatient for Summer

With a seasonal pun, Merri Moser sends a greeting that includes a tiny gift, *above*. To make a holder for the seed packet, Merri cut a slit in the card front just wide enough to slip the packet through. She tied the packet with a length of raffia and then slipped it into the opening, securing it with tape on the back.

Design by Merri Moser

Stars and Stripes Forever

Embellishments make these Fourth of July cards, *right,* a snap to put together: The *Scrapbooks etc.* staff made them in minutes. The rustic style of the front flag card was achieved by gluing pieces of white and blue card stock to the front of a red card and adding star-shape buttons. The center card features a string of star-shape beads threaded through holes pierced in the front panel and tied on the back. The back card has a cutout window in the front panel that reveals the beaded flag sticker inside.

Designs by the Scrapbooks etc. *staff*

JUST FOR DAD

This very masculine-looking card by Renee Villalobos-Campa for her dad features trinkets such as washers and a pocket-watch charm, patterned paper with vintage pop-bottle caps, jute, and a highly textured handmade paper. Renee made the "dad" title with a font she printed in reverse on card stock and then cut out. She used an engraving tool to achieve the weathered, wavy edges.

Design by Renee Villalobos-Campa

Manly Masterpieces

A trio of Father's Day cards, *right,* by Kathleen Paneitz and Polly Maly offers best wishes to Dad on his special day. The card on the left includes stamped and embossed leaves and lettering in warm copper on earth-toned card stock. The torn panel is attached to the card with small brass brads and a hemp-bow accent. The playful card in the center includes plastic mesh, buttons, and colorful fibers for an artistic touch. The word "Dad" can be computer- or hand-printed before attaching to the ring tag. At right, the sepia-tone photo of a father and his children is accented by a rustic tin heart on a wire. The text below the photo reads, "Before you stole their hearts," and inside is another photo of the children's mother and the rest of the message: "you stole mine."

Designs by Kathleen Paneitz and Polly Maly

The Pitter-Patter of Little Feet

A stamp of his little one's footprint will send a message straight to any dad's heart, *below.* Polly Maly used white paint to image the footprint onto dark blue card stock. She let the paint dry and then trimmed and mounted the piece on light blue card stock. The message, printed on vellum, is attached with colored brads in each corner. The piece is adhered to white card stock.

Design by Polly Maly

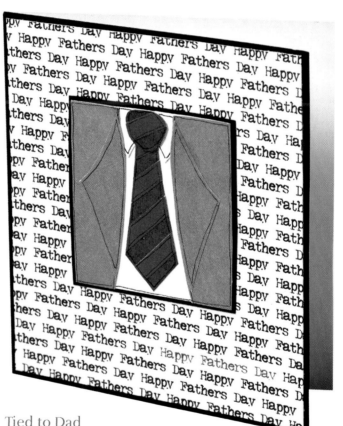

Tied to Dad

A pieced shirt, tie, and jacket in white, red, and blue and a computer-printed background express Christina Cole's sentiments to her father on this card, *above.* Christina used red card stock and dark red patterned paper to create the tie stripes and outlined all the pieces to give them definition. Patterns begin on page 92.

Design by Christina Cole

autumn

SHARED BLESSINGS

A sewing machine and several harvest-hue papers were the tools that Jennifer Ditz McGuire used to make this Thanksgiving card. The background is a piece of cream card stock, layered with gold and rust card stock and patterned paper. Jennifer used a machine zigzag stitch to join the colored papers before attaching them to the background card stock. More layers of card stock and patterned paper hold a rubber-stamped leaf and a faux wax seal. Alphabet stamps spell out the word "Blessings."

Design by Jennifer Ditz McGuire

Jack-o'-Buttons Card

Making this stitched card, *above*, takes no special skills, according to the *Scrapbooks etc.* staff. They simply wrote "Happy Halloween!" on the front panel of a cream card and stitched over the text with orange floss. Three orange buttons are threaded with floss in the lower right corner, with a green stem stitched above each. To finish, they cut two rectangular windows in a piece of green card stock and fit the paper over the stitched elements.

Design by the Scrapbooks etc. *staff*

Halloween Masks

Vertical slits cut in the front of these cards, *below,* make it easy to slip in a colorful Halloween picture. To make the picture enclosure, the *Scrapbooks etc.* staff stamped the masks on a piece of card stock with black ink and heat-embossed them with black embossing powder. Using an artist's brush to apply bleach to the masks created a lighter area. Once the ink was dry, staff members used colored pencils to color the faces. The left and right sides of the card stock were torn and slid through the slits in the front panel of the backing. To make the saying, they slid a long ⅜-inch-wide strip of card stock into a manual label maker, winding and tucking the excess card stock into the handle. "Happy Halloween" is embossed across the strip and attached to the front panel with mini brads.

Designs by the Scrapbooks etc. *staff*

Ghostly Notes

Heidi Boyd accented her clever and "punny" Halloween cards, *below,* with shrink-plastic figures on the card fronts. Before putting the shapes in the oven to shrink them, she used markers to draw the details. (To shrink the shapes, she followed the manufacturer's instructions.) To attach the shapes to the card, she punched two holes through all paper layers and threaded the ends of a rubber band through the holes. After the shrunken pieces had cooled, Heidi tucked each shape through the rubber-band loops. Patterns begin on page 92.

Designs by Heidi Boyd

Sheer Beauty

This card duo by Jennifer Ditz McGuire encourages her friends to achieve their full potential. Gently looped sheer ribbons form wings or petals when paired with a wrapped butterfly body or a button flower center. On the flower card, Jennifer used embroidery floss to sew the looped ribbon and button to the card background and then formed a stem from green ribbon. The butterfly's body is made from paper raffia wrapped with light blue ribbon. Jennifer tied the ribbon ends in a knot at one end of the body and trimmed the ends to make antennae. Several colors of ribbon, folded back and forth, form the butterfly's wings. Stamped messages play off of the motifs.

Designs by Jennifer Ditz McGuire

ANY Occasion

If it's the thought that counts, then sending a

handmade card anytime you think about a friend or family member

is always the right thing to do.

...YOU can FLY...

...BLOOM

where you are PLANTED..

Call on Nature

Donna Downey looked to themes from nature when she created these simple any-occasion cards, *right*. To make the hangtags, she placed small dried flowers in the center of one tag and a butterfly embellishment on the other. The tags are hung from a band of matching ribbon.

Designs by Donna Downey

Set Your Spirit Free

Leftover scraps of paper and three types of spray paints were chosen by Lori Bergmann to make her beach-inspired card, *below right*. After spraying white card stock with stained-glass paint and letting it dry, she added clouds to the sky with a stippling brush dipped in white ink. She also tore two strips of card stock sprayed with stone-finish paint and layered them at the bottom of the card for the sand dunes. The starfish die cut was sprayed with suede-finish paint to give it a mottled look.

Design by Lori Bergmann

Turn Toward the Sun

This trifold card by Jennifer Ditz McGuire, *below*, basks in the glow of a sunny day. Jennifer crafted the sun by poking a needle-hole outline through the layered papers and backstitching with yellow embroidery floss through the holes. To make the raffia closure, she threaded one end of the raffia through the hole in the back section, creating an 8-inch-long tail. She threaded the opposite end of the raffia through holes in the center and front card sections; the raffia is knotted to close the card.

Design by Jennifer Ditz McGuire

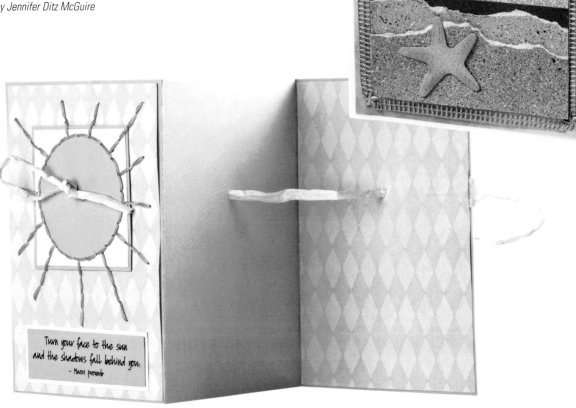

SOFT SQUARES

Watercolors make it simple to create custom cards for any occasion. Here, Nichol Magouirk used watercolor pencils to draw a softly focused block pattern on a sheet of white card stock and to stamp the flower pattern. She also tinted the mini envelope and stamped its tag with a simple stamped sentiment. The tag is attached to the envelope with a string to keep it from being lost. The envelope is glued to the front of the card and embellished with a metal flower and mini brad.

Design by Nichol Magouirk

Golden Thoughts

Metallic leafing and richly colored vellum jazz up translucent stickers on these cards, *above*, by Stephanie Scheetz. Stephanie pressed leafing flakes into the adhesive-sticker backing, rubbing softly but firmly with her fingers and using scissors to clean up the edges. She wrapped gold cord around one of the stickers before adhering it to add interest. Then she adhered the stickers to colored vellum and attached them to the card fronts. One of the cards is finished with a saying stamped on a piece of vellum and embossed with gold powder.

Designs by Stephanie Scheetz

Gold and Silver Treasure

To make the tile accent on this card, *left*, Lori Bergmann mixed modeling paste with paint and applied several thin coats to a square of chipboard. Lori then applied a thicker coat and added a bit more paint in random spots, blending it with a palette knife. She went over the piece with a heat tool until it was only slightly tacky and then pressed a dampened rubber stamp into the tile, leaving it in place until the piece had cooled completely. Gold Rub 'n Buff was worked into the design before the tile was mounted on the card front.

Design by Lori Bergmann

A MINI FLOWER

To make the tiny flower motif on this card, Suzanne Slate stamped the image on a sheet of frosted shrink plastic with black ink and then used permanent markers to color in the design before shrinking. After baking it according to the manufacturer's directions, Suzanne applied a clear acrylic top coat for shine. She wrapped the square with thin gold wire and adhered it to the card with double-stick tape. A tip from Suzanne: The key to successfully using shrink plastic is to think small. If you use an 8½-inch sheet of plastic for your design, the finished piece will be only about 4 inches long. Plan ahead by making your designs about two times larger than you want them to appear when finished.

Design by Suzanne Slate

A Bloomin' Beauty

To brighten a friend's day, Erika Clayton used punched petals, leaves, and circles to form flowers on a bright backing of pink, green, and white, *above*. After punching holes with a needle, she threaded ribbon through the holes and tied a soft bow. To complete the card, she cut narrow pink card-stock strips to form a stripe pattern on the inside bottom edge.

Design by Erika Clayton

Stylized Sunshine

This sophisticated card, *above right,* features a shrink-plastic element suspended from silver cord in a custom-cut window. Veronica Koh created the piece by rubber-stamping the image on shrink plastic that she'd already painted with metallic paint and punching two $\frac{1}{4}$-inch holes at the top and bottom. After the plastic was baked according to the manufacturer's instructions, Veronica took it out of the oven and lightly spooned clear embossing powder over the piece in a thin layer. Then she put it back in the oven again for about 2 minutes, to melt the powder and create a rough, textured surface.

Design by Veronica Koh

A Transparent Message

Transparencies are great to pair with rub-on letters and graphics. To prove it, Anita Matejka created this card, *right,* by adhering rub-ons to a small piece of transparency film and attaching the transparency to the back of a green window. She used adhesive foam to mount the combination over the flower die cut for a dimensional effect.

Design by Anita Matejka

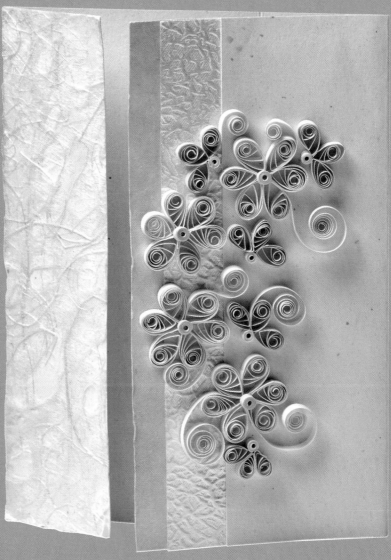

GRACEFUL SWIRLS AND WHIRLS

Quilling—rolling strips of paper around a needle tool or pin—forms intricate designs on this delicate card by Laurel Albright. To quill the papers to form her design, Laurel secured one end of the strip of paper around the tool by pinching it in place. She rolled the handle of the tool between her thumb and fingers to create a circle with the paper strip. When finished, she secured the loose end to the inner edge with a dab of clear-drying glue and pressed it until dry. To create shapes, she lightly pinched the pieces between her fingers. Patterns begin on page 92.

Design by Laurel Albright

THANKS
for everything

A handcrafted card is a gracious acknowledgment of the good deeds performed by friends and acquaintances.

A CARD WITH A LITTLE EXTRA

A pouch card, *opposite*, does double duty: saying "Thank You" and providing a place to stash candy, potpourri, or another tiny thank-you treat. Erin Terrell cut a 5×12-inch length of heavy card stock and scored lines at 4, 7, and 11 inches. She set eyelets just below the 11-inch fold. With a clear-drying adhesive, she attached decorative fibers to the front panel and flap. A flower template provided the base for the daisy; Erin finished it off with a bright yellow button sewn onto the center. To hold the treats inside, she cut a small paper sack to fit after folding the box to hold it. Erin attached the daisy to the flap and a stamped tag and ribbon to the pouch front to complete the card.

Design by Erin Terrell

Thank You for Coming

Present each of your guests with a small accordion-fold thank-you booklet at the party's conclusion as a take-home gift, *above*. The cover is a die-cut element that fits the party theme, and the inside is filled with digital snapshots taken during the day and printed while the guests enjoyed themselves.

Design by Anita Matejka

Thanks a Bunch

A sincere "Thanks" embossed over and over on the front of this card, *left,* lets the recipient know how much he or she is appreciated. Anita Matejka typed the word in several different fonts on a sheet of white paper. She placed the paper on a sheet of foam core with cut pieces of light blue and green vellum in between. Then, using a stylus, she embossed the words onto the vellum. Anita adhered the vellum panels to the card and secured the corners with brads to complete her card.

Design by Anita Matejka

STAMPED WITH PUNCH

Amy Lowe credits her square alphabet shadow stamps for the punch packed by her thank-you card, *below*. Amy says, "I knew that I could use them to get nice square shadow images, but for this card I wanted circles. So I stamped a word as I would normally and then punched the letters out with a small circle punch." Her stamps give a hint of texture that printer ink never could, and the negative-space lettering gives the illusion of reverse-type printing without using too much color-printer ink.

Design by Amy Lowe

Cheery Thoughts

Sunny colors and an eye-popping posy will brighten anyone's day, *opposite, top left*. For dimensional texture, Kathleen Paneitz filled a three-dimensional keeper with beads (nonpareils work also). Using a large oval punch, she cut the sunflower petals and lightly chalked the petal edges. The petals overlap on the card front, and the keeper fills the flower's center. To finish the card, she wrapped raffia twists around the corners and adhered them to the underside of the card front.

Design by Kathleen Paneitz

Thanks for making my day so bright

The Leather Look

"I love the look of leather on scrapbook pages and cards, but I didn't want to have to invest in a whole new set of tools to try my hand at leather-working. So I came up with a great way to fake the look of leather with crafts foam, a heat-embossing tool, and metallic rub-on pigment," Teri Anderson says. To make the card, *above*, she heated a piece of white crafts foam with a heat-embossing tool for about a minute, until the foam softened and the edges started to curl. She inked a stamp with watermark ink and pressed it into the foam for about a minute; replenished the stamp with a black dye ink, and re-pressed it into the same position. She let the foam cool and the ink dry for another minute and then used her finger to color the foam with metallic rub-on pigment. Teri notes that brown, black, bronze, and red pigments work well with this process.

Design by Teri Anderson

A Marbleized Jewel

Rich colors, a sparkling greeting, and graceful shapes say "thank you" brilliantly, *left*. Jan Achiu punched decorative corners in the blue-marbled paper before mounting it on a backing of silver foil board. She stamped an expression of thanks on an oval of dark blue card stock. While the ink was still wet, Jan applied diamond sparkle powder and heat-embossed it. After drying, she attached the "thank-you" oval to the right card panel and a window oval to the left so that the "thank-you" piece slips through the window to close the card.

Design by Jan Achiu

Heartfelt Thanks

Soft felt on the front gives textural focus to Alison Beachem's thank-you card, *above.* Alison used a personal die cutter to make the felt flowers. Then she hand-cut the leaves, stitched detailing on the leaves and flower centers, and adhered the finished flowers to the front panel, securing a ribbon beneath them at the top to tie the card closed.

Design by Alison Beachem

A Blooming Thank-You

Buttons, crafts wire, raffia, and twine help this thank-you card by Polly McMillan, *above right,* bloom with texture and creativity. Her punched flowerpots hold punched posies and leaves; she made tiny holes in the flowers to correspond with the buttons and tied them onto the flowers with twine. Bent crafts wire forms the stems, which are mounted behind the flowers and pots. A handwritten thank-you note shaded with chalk appears below the pots. Layers of raffia, gathered beneath a button, ground the pots and the note. The button is secured to the raffia with twine.

Design by Polly McMillan

Thanks in Any Language

To make this unconventional card, *right,* Polly Maly typed "thank you" in multiple languages and printed the words on white card stock. She attached the printed sheet to white mat board and covered it with sheer fabric, which she secured to the back with tape. She added the ribbon and metal flower paper-clip embellishment and attached the piece to the card's front panel.

Design by Polly Maly

Simply Grateful

This neatly geometric card in muted shades of green is easy to make, according to Teresa Snyder. Layers of coordinating green papers and black card stock form the background for the sticker letters, which were mounted on vellum. She attached the vellum with silver eyelets and finished the card with punched white daisies.

Design by Teresa Snyder

FLUTTERING BY TO SAY THANKS

A small punched window surrounded by contrasting colors frames the focal-point butterfly in this understated card by Jami Blackham. The final motif is a combination of three punched butterflies: one each punched in blue, pink, and vellum. Jami trimmed the wings from the blue butterfly, adhered the vellum to the pink butterfly along the body, and glued the blue body to the center of the wings. She mounted the butterfly on the small purple square and pulled up the wings for added dimension.

Design by Jami Blackham

LOVE *always*

Let that special someone in your life know just how much

he or she means to you with a message straight from your heart.

HUGS AND KISSES

If love is a never-ending circle, then Tracy Kyle's card, *opposite*, with its three large graphic spheres is the perfect symbol. Tracy cut circles of coordinating patterned paper and attached them to a card stock base, and then she cut coordinating border strips from card stock. She finished the card with ribbons and a printed tag.

Design by Tracy Kyle

Rose Garden

The simple beauty and repetition of this hearts-and-flowers grid, *above*, came from a template Arlene Santos designed using a corner punch to notch each square block. The card layers include ridged textured paper and silver foil paper; she cut the grid pattern from pink rose-pattern vellum. After notching the cut vellum, she wrapped each block with silver metallic thread; the tiny indentations make wrapping the threads easy. Her final layering included punched silver hearts topped with floral stickers.

Design by Arlene Santos

A Dangling Heart

A bit of waxed string ties a heart charm to a bright gingham-ribbon bow on this card by Michelle Keith, *left*. A background of script-patterned paper matted in silver and pink highlights the heart against the brown card stock. Preprinted ribbon spells out the all-important message.

Design by Michelle Keith

you're always
in my heart

Say It with Flowers

To create her own epoxylike stickers, Shannon Landen glued dried flowers to a page protector (a transparency also would work) and covered them with dimensional glue, using a punched card stock template to keep the glue in a circular shape, *above*. After removing the template, Shannon filled in the center portion of each circle with more glue to cover the flower, adding multiple layers. When the glue was dry, she cut out her "pebbles" and added a flower sticker to the back of each one, followed by a layer of glue to make the flowers look as though they're floating.

Design by Shannon Landen

A Part of My Heart

Vivian Smith shares an expression straight from her heart with the cutout card, *above right*, which frames a heart sticker. The front of the card features geometric cutouts in patterned paper.

Design by Vivian Smith

A Gift of Love

Sometimes the simplest expressions are the most eloquent. A sticker dresses up the plain white card designed by the *Scrapbooks etc.* staff, *right*. The text on the card is computer-printed but would be extra special if it were handwritten. There's room inside for a personalized message.

Design by the Scrapbooks etc. *staff*

YOUR LOVE IS
THE BEST GIFT
I'VE EVER
BEEN GIVEN

BED OF ROSES

A stark black-and-white photo sticker and a black word block contrast with the creamy, romantic paper and delicate ribbon on this dreamy card. Renee Foss lightly sanded the images and rubbed them with a soft pink ink pad. She then stamped a tapestry motif onto the card stock with watermark ink, embossed it with clear embossing powder, and tore it into a narrow strip to create the subtle background paper behind the image. After mounting the matted sticker and word block with adhesive foam, she finished by dragging the four edges along the pink ink pad and adding a ribbon strung with beads to the card front along the folded edge.

Design by Renee Foss

DOTTY FOR YOU

A profusion of red-and-white polka dots boldly trumpets an "I love you" message from Cara Mariano on this four-panel accordion-fold card. The message is framed by a series of progressively smaller die-cut hearts centered on the brightly papered panels. Her message appears on the smallest, innermost heart.

Design by Cara Mariano

Circle of Love

The message on Veronica Koh's card, *top left*, forms a never-ending circle. Punching holes in both the front and back of the card creates a clear window for the dangling gingham heart she attached to the inside. Veronica punched two gingham hearts and glued them together, sandwiching the hanging thread in between.

Design by Veronica Koh

Colorful Collage

Vibrant fibers, ribbons, and gold paint give Shannon Landen's collage-inspired card, *below left,* a personality of its own. To stamp the swirled design onto red velvet, Shannon placed an inked stamp faceup on an ironing board. With the velvet on top, she held a heated iron against the fabric. The card stock base glistens with the shimmer of gold acrylic paint. To finish the card, she added stickers, fabric flowers, and gold buttons.

Design by Shannon Landen

Bold and Beautiful

Grabbing attention in the center of the silk flower, *below,* is a faux-wax seal brushed with paint to bring out the detail. Nichol Magouirk secured metallic ribbon behind the flower and placed a black metal-rim tag just under one of the petals. Finally, she inked the edges of a definition sticker and secured it with colored staples.

Design by Nichol Magouirk

Stamped with Love

Square and heart-shape punches and paper edgers earn this card, *above left*, our stamp of approval. To make the pattern, Kathleen Paneitz punched two squares each from plum and pink card stock and then centered and adhered them to a background of white card stock. She punched one heart each from pink and plum card stock, layered them and cut them into quarters, and alternated the colors as she attached them to the background checkerboard. The letters were cut with a lettering template, and the price is made from stickers.

Design by Kathleen Paneitz

A Window to My Heart

Veronica Koh's messenger card, *above right*, sports a square punched in the front and a dainty punched heart held taut with gold thread. Sewing the thread through both sides of the heart and both sides of the card front and then tying it in a knot on the back of the card front holds the heart securely in place.

Design by Veronica Koh

Committed to Us

A photo of the happy couple shines from the front of this card, *right,* by Julie Medeiros. She attached the photo with photo corners and used a definition sticker and a seal to proclaim that her dreams have been fulfilled. She finished the card with a heart clip.

Design by Julie Medeiros

So hung up on you!

SO "CLOTHES" TO YOU

Kathleen Paneitz proves that a demonstration of
true love doesn't always have to be mushy and
serious: A dose of humor works, too. Layers of card
stock and mulberry paper frame the tiny hanger she
shaped from fine gold wire and its punched metal
heart. (She punched a hole in the heart and
threaded the wire through it before forming the
hanger.) To attach the hanger to the card, she poked
tiny needle holes in the paper and secured the
hanger with fine wire twisted on the back.

Design by Kathleen Paneitz

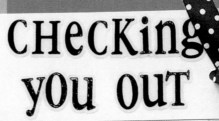

CHECKING YOU OUT

DATE	ISSUED TO
12/24	While you were putting presents under the tree
12/31	At Jenny's New Year's party

Sweetheart,

I made this card in honor of all the times I've checked you out recently. You're looking good, hot stuff! ♥

KEEPING AN EYE ON YOU

Just to let her special someone know that she's always looking out for him, Candi Gershon crafted a library-theme card. A library-card pocket holds a computer-printed "checkout" card containing a list of times Candi noticed her guy in action. Her handwritten explanation appears on the front of the pocket. She mounted stamped hearts beside the pocket to complete the card.

Design by Candi Gershon

Soul Mates

Very basic materials combine to form this meaningful card from Lisa Stephenson, *top left*. Starting with a favorite photo, Lisa added rub-on letters, a preprinted phrase, a label holder, and a heart charm to express her feelings.

Design by Lisa Stephenson

Valentine Spin Game

Children will enjoy the thrill of a special Valentine treat or two—in addition to the fun of receiving a card—when they open the envelope of the Spin Game card, *below left*. Candi Gershon layered background papers and a circle and then stamped on the possible rewards. The purchased spinner is attached with a brad.

Design by Candi Gershon

Our Two Hearts

Without a written word, the front of this card, *below*, gets its point across: Our two hearts beat as one. Erika Clayton used gold and yellow card stocks for richness and added an overlay of vellum and a luxurious ribbon for romantic flair.

Design by Erika Clayton

Eyes for Love

A large collection of eyelets was Shannon Landen's inspiration for making this special card, *far right*. First, she adhered seven 1-inch strips of patterned paper and vellum to a folded sheet of card stock. Using a heart-shape die cut as a guide, she made pencil marks on the card front to indicate the positions of her eyelets and set them, nesting each inside a washer. Dry-brushed gold paint in the center of the heart and rub-on words and letter pebbles complete the card.

Design by Shannon Landen

Lavender Lovely

A pretty pastel pattern paper is the background for this lovely card, *right*, created by Donna Downey. The word "love" is framed in a silver charm, and two silver eyelets are threaded with a purple cord tie.

Design by Donna Downey

Lots of Love

Die cuts don't have to be from the same company or of the same design to work well together. Anita Matejka chose hearts from her die cut and sticker collection to create the special card, *right*. She painted a few hearts blue to coordinate with the other die cuts and layered everything on the card front. She also added metal letters to spell out "love" at the bottom of the card and wrapped a length of tulle around the card at the top fold.

Design by Anita Matejka

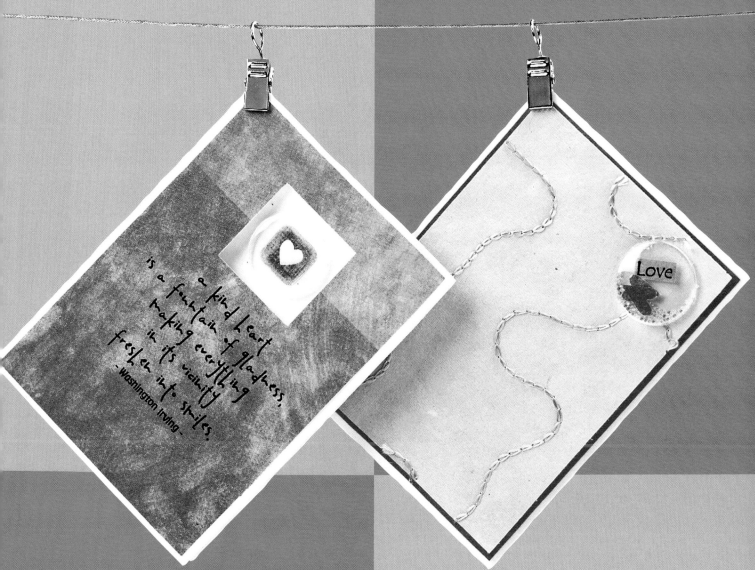

MY LOVE IS MAGNIFIED

Watch crystals magnify the motifs tucked beneath
them, bringing three-dimensional appeal to these
lovely cards. Jennifer Ditz McGuire cautions to
carefully size your stamps, wording, and other motifs
so they don't spill out from under the domes. She
used Diamond Glaze glue to attach the crystals to
the papers.

The "Love" card, *right,* includes hearts punched
from scrap paper and a few beads adhered inside the
crystal. One of the papers layered beneath is stitched
for texture.

The "kind heart" card, *left,* features a square
window punched in the card front. Beneath the
watch crystal is a simple heart sticker.

Designs by Jennifer Ditz McGuire

YOU'RE
invited

Any cause for celebration deserves a stellar invitation. Let your imagination soar—and match the tone of your invitation to the special event you're planning.

Charm Your Friends

Gold-checked ribbon and a fanciful charm dress up this New Year's Eve party invitation by Jennifer Ditz McGuire, *above*. Jennifer stamped the ribbon with her message and threaded a charm onto the horizontal band before securing the ends with tape.

Design by Jennifer Ditz McGuire

Black-Tie Affair

A dressy invitation let Kristin Detrick's guests know in advance that her New Year's party would be a formal event, *left*. Kristin used black moiré card stock and star-print vellum as the base. To make the bow tie, she cut 5-inch and 12-inch lengths of $\frac{5}{8}$-inch ribbon, a 5-inch length of $\frac{3}{8}$-inch ribbon, and a 4-inch length of crafts wire. She folded the 5-inch length of $\frac{5}{8}$-inch ribbon in the center, overlapping the ends about $\frac{1}{2}$ inch, and secured it to the center of the 12-inch ribbon with wire. The $\frac{3}{8}$-inch ribbon was tied around the wire to hide it and to form the bow knot. She finished the tie by trimming the ribbon and taping the tails to the 12-inch ribbon.

Design by Kristin Detrick

Offer a Toast

Silver, gold, and swirl-print vellum pair with gold card stock and a slender champagne flute in this urbane party invitation by Gabriella Hunter, *below left*. She printed party details on silver vellum to fit inside the glass shape and cut the flute from a pattern. Circles of different sizes punched from gold and silver vellum "float" on the card to represent bubbles. Gabriella used a lettering template to cut the gold-vellum numbers. She added a small length of wire holding a punched circle to serve as a wine charm. Patterns begin on page 92.

Design by Gabriella Hunter

10, 9, 8 ...

Fun, tactile elements combine on this invitation by Natasha Roe, *below*. Plastic letters, a die paper clip, and "buckled" ribbons join a vellum-pieced champagne glass that's stitched onto the front. Patterns begin on page 92.

Design by Natasha Roe

In the Bag

Sleeping bags and pillows are must-haves for a sleepover party (even if the guests don't use them for sleeping), so Jennifer Beaman incorporated the essentials into her slumber-party invitation, *left*. She cut a bag front and back and then matted the front with black card stock and trim, leaving a thin border. The bag back was adhered to the front to secure the edges, but the top was left open for slipping in a text card. Jennifer added a turned-down edge piece and computer-printed the party information on a strip of card stock that she attached to the matted pillow. The pillow details were outlined with a black marker. Patterns begin on page 92.

Design by Jennifer Beaman

Pretty in Pink

A cute pink purse carries a sweet invitation to a little girl's party, *below left*. Debi Adams used a purchased template to cut a pattern from white vellum and stitched the pieces together, leaving the top open. Stamped and heat-embossed daisies decorate the purse front, and the bold pink handle is adorned with flower buttons (stickers would work, too). Tucked inside the purse is an invitation embellished with pink matting, a button, and a snippet of ribbon.

Design by Debi Adams

Top It Off

A party-hat laser-cut takes center stage on this invitation designed by the *Scrapbooks etc.* staff, *below*. They glued the laser-cut to white card stock and cut away the card around the top of the hat on both the front and back. The number is cut from patterned paper using a template, and the text is lettered with markers.

Design by the Scrapbooks etc. *staff*

You're Invited...
For Gavin's 3rd Birthday Party
time 11:00 am
date Sat. Sept 30th
place Blank Park Zoo - Snow Monkey deck
rsvp Wed. Sept 27th

IT'S A JUNGLE OUT THERE

The giraffe pattern stamped onto the front of this party invitation gives a broad hint as to the location of the party ... with the lions, tigers, and giraffes, of course! Makyla Iverson created the invitation for her son's third birthday party. She stamped the giraffe pattern on layered card stock for the front and created an animal-stamped foldout inside with the party details.

Design by Makyla Iverson

Diaper Duty

A piece of a real cloth diaper embellishes Nichol Magouirk's baby-shower invitation, *right*. Patterned paper and vellum are stitched to a card-stock backing; the text is computer-printed on coordinating paper. Nichol snipped a swatch from a cloth diaper and folded it into a diaper shape, matted the diaper onto patterned paper, and secured it with a safety-pin nailhead.

Design by Nichol Magouirk

Rock-a-Bye Baby

Planning the text around the graphic element is key to the success of this baby-shower announcement, *below right,* created by Shannon Smith. Shannon printed the invitation on white card stock, leaving gaps between the text lines at the center of the announcement. Stamping the horse image with dye ink over the text was her next step. The invitation slips neatly into a vellum envelope embellished with a purple bow in the center.

Design by Shannon Smith

Preview Present

The tiny package on the front of this invitation, *below,* hints at a special day filled with good things. Stephanie Scheetz constructed the package out of mat board wrapped in pink vellum that was stamped with a pattern. The package is accented with pretty ribbon, attached to the card with double-stick tape, and finished with a sticker gift tag.

Design by Stephanie Scheetz

Twinkle Twinkle Little Star

Twinkle Twinkle Little Star
how we wonder who you are.
Come join us for a baby
shower for Susan and
her new shining star
November 12
at 1:00 pm
24232 Milky Way Drive
Starburst, CA 92220

SHINING STAR

Cara Mariano chose the design of this card—made almost entirely of die cuts—because it is so easy to mass-produce. Cara's first step was to die-cut the peekaboo portion of the card on cream card stock, folding it along the crease lines. The card is constructed in layers, with light green on the bottom, topped with a layer of striped paper, and crowned with a star. The information is printed on vellum, which is positioned over the layers. The layers are inserted into the card and taped into place, leaving the flap loose. The card flap is matted with layers of card stock; the top cream layer has "Twinkle Twinkle Little Star" printed on it. The moon and star are die-cut, and the circles are punched.

Design by Cara Mariano

SET THE ALARM!

It's important not to let time slip away without seeing good friends often. That's why the *Scrapbooks etc.* staff designed this simple contemporary invitation to call for a gathering of friends. Cut circles are attached to a card-stock front, running off the sides for an in-a-hurry feel. The clock face is a large ring tag; the hands are cut from card stock and held on with a mini brad. Adhesive foam holds the clock face to the background.

Design by the Scrapbooks etc. *staff*

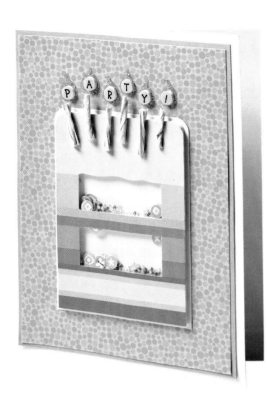

Time for a Disguise

A nose-and-glasses disguise from a novelty shop inspired Vicky Breslin and Lindsay Ostrom to put together the clever masquerade-party invitation, *above*. They simply glued the novelty to layered Halloween-color papers, printed the message on vellum, cut it out, and glued it to the card front. Party details are printed on the inside of the card.

Design by Vicky Breslin and Lindsay Ostrom

Light the Candles

The details on Lori Bergmann's invitation to party, *above left,* will delight recipients. Two windows covered in Mylar (plastic would work, too) showcase tiny stickers and seed beads, and mini raffia candles top the "cake." Lori used a template to cut a rectangle with two windows in striped card stock and also in white craft foam. She glued a square of clear Mylar to the back side of the window openings in the card stock and matted the foam on white card stock. To fill the windows, she attached stickers to small punched circles of white card stock and placed the stickers and seed beads into the recesses in the foam. Then she glued the striped card stock to the foam to seal the shaker and mounted the piece on the card front. Twisted lengths of pink raffia form the candles, and alphabet stickers invite the recipient to come party.

Design by Lori Bergmann

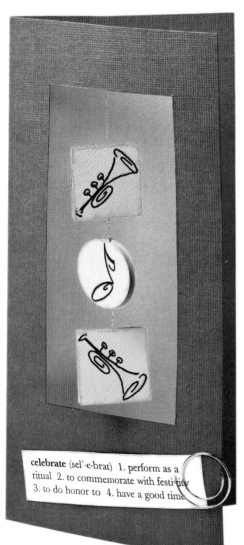

A Jazzy Invite

This invitation by Melissa Inman, *left*, hits a high note even before the upcoming celebration. Melissa used rubber stamps to make the instruments, although she says that stickers would work well, too. The rubber stamps she used for this project were a little too big for the punched shapes she wanted, so Melissa stamped the images on a sheet of white paper and scanned them into her computer. Then she resized each image to fit her shapes and printed them on card stock.

To suspend the images, Melissa cut a window in the card large enough to house the shapes in the front panel. She sandwiched a length of thread between the shapes, using adhesive foam to join the two sides. The pieces are suspended in the window by attaching the string to the inside with transparent tape. A piece of cut card stock the same size as the front panel covers the tape.

Design by Melissa Inman

Invitación de la Fiesta

Cinco de Mayo, or Fifth of May, is a happy, colorful Mexican holiday. To match the spirit of the day, Mary Jo Hiney designed this colorful serape-style invitation for her festivities, *left*. The base of the card is covered with bright stripes of card stock, which are overlapped and glued to the front of the card. The text is formed from letter stickers, and the card is topped with a tan card-stock sombrero. Patterns begin on page 92.

Design by Mary Jo Hiney

A Sizzling Celebration

Merri Moser served up her barbeque-party invitation, *below left,* in a red-and-white-check napkin. She printed the party details on white card stock, matted it onto red card stock, and folded a napkin jacket to hold the card. She taped the jacket at the overlap to hold it together and tied on a piece of raffia to finish the invitation.

Design by Merri Moser

Latkes, Laughter, and Lights

A meaningful quote inspired this invitation by Susan Badgett, *below,* that invites guests to join in the family's Hanukkah celebrations. Vellum cut to resemble a house stands in the foreground, and nine candles in varying sizes and shades of blue rest on the silver background. To add interest, Susan slanted the candles slightly. The vellum house is attached with silver mini brads. Patterns begin on page 92.

Design by Susan Badgett

"To invite a person to your house is to take charge of their happiness for as long as he is under your roof."

a. Brillat-Savarin

Join the Friedmans for Latkes, Laughter, and Lights as we celebrate the first night of Hanukkah.

Where: 1727 Terrace Hills Way
When: December 19 at 5:30 p.m.

We would love
for you to join us in

celebrating the
joys of the season

Saturday, December 6,
six o'clock p.m.
at the home of Ken & Jennifer
367 Tradwinds Drive, Montgomery
RSVP regrets only

INFORMAL HOLIDAY GATHERING

With a casual invitation like this one from Jennifer Ditz McGuire, there's no need to explain that it's not a formal affair. Mismatched buttons and a handmade paper star, tucked under a swatch of plaid fabric, set the stage for an easygoing get-together. The text is printed on clear transparency and mounted on textured paper and rose card stock.

Design by Jennifer Ditz McGuire

TEA-TIME CHARMER

This folded-pouch card by Laura Collins is steeped in beads, buttons, lacy ribbon, and a sample of the featured tea. Laura printed the card on vellum and folded it as a pouch to hold a plastic bag filled with the tea. She printed the name of the tea on lavender card stock to which she attached a charm. An 8-inch length of wire strung with seed and faceted beads connects the tiny card to the pouch. Laura attached the wire to the pouch through two holes punched in the top of the card. Patterns begin on page 92.

Design by Laura Collins

Happy Housewarming

Fabrics are woven into the theme of Nicole Gartland's '50s-inspired house-warming invitation, *right*. Nicole rubber-stamped her greeting on a piece of eyelet lace and wrapped it around the card front. She added another piece of scallop-edge ribbon to the figure of the woman and tied a ribbon bow at the waist to simulate an apron. Patterns begin on page 92.

Design by Nicole Gartland

Family Gathering

A family reunion is a special event deserving of a beautiful card like the one, *below right*. For this reunion invitation, Erikia Ghumm used a custom-made rubber stamp and sepia ink to imprint an image of her grandmother on tan card stock. She tore out the stamped image, chalked it to give it a hand-tinted appearance, and adhered it to a tag with a stamped background.

Design by Erikia Ghumm

50 Years and Counting

The central theme of this 50th-anniversary-celebration invitation, *below,* is the love that has withstood the test of time. Cindy Knowles folded the card stock and printed the outside text; the inside text was computer-printed on colored vellum and inserted into the card. Cindy cut the "Love" letters from gold card stock using a lettering template, matted them with green card stock, and adhered them to the front panels. She let the letter O overlap the right panel of the card and added a rose sticker to its center.

Design by Cindy Knowles

Giving Thanks

Warm tones on this invitation, *left*, set the stage for a celebration of autumn's bounty hosted by Kathleen Paneitz. She computer-printed the text and used card stock in brown, tan, and burgundy to capture the mood. Raffia, square eyelets, and gingham ribbon add texture; a purchased turkey embellishment underscores the Thanksgiving theme.

Design by Kathleen Paneitz

A Simple Thanksgiving

Autumn's colorful palette inspired this invitation by Alison Beachem, *below left*. Inside, details are computer-printed on a plain piece of neutral card stock; out front "Thanksgiving" is printed using stickers. Alison added a border, leaf stickers, and bronze mini brads and then she set two eyelets in each flap at the overlap to secure the ribbon that holds the card closed.

Design by Alison Beachem

Visit Our "Web Site"

A fuzzy spider made from a pom-pom adds personality to Jennie Dayley's invitation to a Halloween party, *below*. The hole in the front is large enough for the spider to peek through yet remain in place when the card is opened. The border is paper cut with pinking shears; the details are printed with a marker. Patterns begin on page 92.

Design by Jennie Dayley

CLASS ASSIGNMENT

Thanksgiving projects are always popular in the classroom; many former students fondly remember cutting out turkeys, coloring cornucopias, or reading about the Pilgrims. To hearken back to schoolhouse days, Erikia Ghumm designed this schoolhouse-theme gatefold invitation that closes with a silk ribbon. On the inside, she used a rubber stamp of traditional school notebook paper to mark the guidelines for the text and inked the details with a calligraphy pen. Adding punched-text squares and leaf cutouts finished the invitation.

Design by Erikia Ghumm

Christmas &

Whether you celebrate Christmas, Hanukkah or another holiday, you'll probably find the winter season a time for great rejoicing. It's a time to gather with family and friends, and definitely a time to share greetings with those we care about, whether they live close by or far away.

Stripe Up a Card

This "Merry Christmas" card by Nichol Magouirk is merry, indeed, with a layer of colorful patterned vellum providing instant impact. To make the tree the center of attention, Nichol started with a metal charm adhered to a red laminate chip. She poured tiny silver beads into a watch crystal and, keeping the watch crystal facedown, applied glue around its rim. Then she placed the chip facedown on the watch crystal with the tree centered inside. A sprightly gingham ribbon and stamped message complete the card.

Design by Nichol Magouirk

Hanukkah *greetings*

Shining Stars

Embossed metallic-look stars and silver plastic mesh make this card shine. Alison Beachem punched the stars out of blue card stock and embossed them with silver powder. The bright background started with cream card stock that she gilded with a silver-leaf pen and shaded with blue chalk. She attached the stars with adhesive foam and layered the strip with vellum and silver plastic mesh before attaching it to the card background. Patterns begin on page 92.

Design by Alison Beachem

Wired for the Holidays

Premade wire lights and trees take all the work out of making these deceptively simple cards created by Erin Terrell, *right*. To make the tree card, she cut circles from self-adhesive metallic papers with a circle cutter and attached them in a random pattern to the card. She attached the trees with fishing line, inserted a silver eyelet at the top of the card, and tied a bow through the eyelet. The bright lightbulbs and red bows on her silver card are attached to the backing through two small holes at the top. She threaded the ribbons through the holes and slid the end of each wire lightbulb under the bow, securing them with fishing line.

Designs by Erin Terrell

Jingling Bells

Happy sounds of the season announce the arrival of this card, *below*. Nikki Krueger attached a row of bells to a white card stock strip using embroidery floss and then attached the strip to the card in the same manner. She added her greeting with rub-on letters.

Design by Nikki Krueger

A MERRY, MERRY CHRISTMAS

Premade ornament-shape buttons look cute just hangin' around on this homespun-look card by Helen Naylor. Helen cut a window in the card stock base and strung a length of wire behind the front of the opening panel. A piece of cream card stock on the inside of the card highlights the buttons that hang from ornament hangers on a piece of stretched wire. Helen adhered the buttons to the card stock to keep them in place and stitched a merry greeting with cotton thread.

Design by Helen Naylor

A CONTEMPORARY CHRISTMAS

A lively mix of patterned papers makes a lighthearted statement on the front of this card by Anita Matejka. An evenly spaced row of brads attached to the card adds instant focus. The metal-word message has a hanger made of embroidery floss.

Design by Anita Matejka

Waiting for Santa

Erin Terrell achieved instant aging on this old-fashioned-look card, *left,* by choosing brown and tan paper colors, inking the edges, and sanding the red paper that frames the Santa sticker. A backing of mesh paper provides additional texture, and the postage-stamp letters stand out, thanks to a backing of adhesive foam. A jute bow adds a final touch of old-world ambience.

Design by Erin Terrell

Home for the Holidays

Nikki Krueger may not make it home for Christmas, but it's clear where her heart is. Her sentimental card, *below,* features a sheet of map-pattern paper on the front. Torn red card stock makes a space for rubber-stamped lettering and a bold "Christmas" label. Nikki added a ribbon around the front of the card by cutting a slit in the top fold, threading the ribbon through the slit, and tying it in a bow.

Design by Nikki Krueger

AN EXTENDED HANUKKAH GREETING

A mantel or tabletop is the perfect spot to display a Hanukkah card that's long on good wishes. Helen Naylor showcased a variety of embellishments and techniques on the nine card stock squares and adhered the decorated squares to long, solid-color backing strips for support. The strips are folded at the point where they attach to the embellished squares. The background candles are made from card stock with twists of wire to hold the flames in place.

Design by Helen Naylor

Ho, Ho, Ho

A paper-pieced Santa is the star of this cheery holiday card, *left*. Helen Naylor started with a pattern to cut the Santa pieces and then chalked in rosy cheeks and inked Santa's black eyes. The figure is double-mounted and adhered to patterned card stock. Helen used letter stamps to spell out her greeting. Patterns begin on page 92.

Design by Helen Naylor

Just "Bleachy"

Helen Naylor used the same stamp to bleach an image on nine card stock squares of different colors for this graphic card, *below*. She layered paper towels in a plastic container and saturated the center of the stack with bleach. Then she dipped the rubber stamp in bleach and applied it to the card stock. Her tips: 1) Bleaching should happen as you press the stamp into the paper; if the action is delayed, use more bleach. 2) Remoisten the paper towels periodically with bleach. 3) Blot the rubber stamp on dry paper towels between stampings to keep bleach from accumulating in crevices, and use a stamp scrubber pad to clean the stamp. 4) Dark papers result in a film-negative look, and lighter paper colors give a more subtle change. 5) Spray with archival mist if the card will be put into an album.

Design by Helen Naylor

A CURLY TREE

A curlicue tree stamp and hand-torn papers are the essentials of this frilly card by Ann E. Young. She used a snowflake stamp on the matting paper, overlapping the images for a lacy look and tearing the background papers to give the card a unique texture. On a separate piece of paper, she stamped and embossed the tree image, tearing the paper around the tree. The tree paper is matted with a hand-torn section of the snowflake paper before the entire design is adhered to the card front.

Design by Ann E. Young

JOY TO THE WORLD

A joyful greeting is the theme of this card by Nichol Magouirk. Nichol tore striped papers to fit the front of a piece of plain card stock, overlapping them slightly and machine-stitching them in place. She attached alphabet stickers to the card and situated conchos over them, pressing the prongs through the card stock and flattening them on the inside front panel.

Design by Nichol Magouirk

Pretty in Pastels

This contemporary card, *left*, by Helen Naylor shines in offbeat, pastel hues. She used patterned paper as a backdrop, but layered papers in blended colors would work as well. The tree form is cut from thin crafts foam; Helen suggests that if you can't find the colors you want, paint white foam pieces with acrylic paints. Her card is finished with punched circles for ornaments and a fabric label with a stitched message. Patterns begin on page 92.

Design by Helen Naylor

Hanging the Ornaments

This playful card, *below*, by Anita Matejka is long on charm, thanks to metal Christmas shapes strung from stripes of colorful floss. Anita began with folded striped card stock and embroidery floss in colors to match the stripes. She backed the charms with card stock and strung them on floss, securing the ends of the floss on the back of the panel. Adhesive holds the charms in place.

Design by Anita Matejka

gift tags

The finishing touch on any wrapped gift is the tag,
so put your creativity to work and make it a mini work of art.

A CHEERY THANK-YOU

Any gift—however small or insignificant—will bloom with a perky gift tag. Kathleen Paneitz wrote
her thank-you message on white card stock and covered it with pink vellum. A punched flower,
swirls, and leaves layer over the pink vellum. A brad fastens the flower pieces to the layers, and
a pink satin ribbon prettily ties the tag to the package.

Design by Kathleen Paneitz

Fairy-Tale Tag

A stash of leftover seed beads was Erin Terrell's inspiration for this gift tag, *right*. She folded a piece of card stock in half and traced a tag shape onto the piece, aligning the bottom edge with the fold. She cut the tag on three sides, leaving the folded edge intact. Then she opened the tag and punched a window through one side. She filled a small clear plastic bag with white seed beads and sealed it shut, taping the bag to the solid back panel of the tag and making sure that the beads showed through the window. Erin finished the tag with embellishments, including strips of pink paper, metal accents, a purchased wire shape, and fabric pieces.

Design by Erin Terrell

For a Music Lover

This "note"-worthy tag by Charla Campbell, *above*, is perfect for a music-related gift. Old sheet music, a torn-paper heart, and two tiny tags with a computer-printed message carry out her theme. The small tags are punched and threaded onto the large tag with gold cord.

Design by Charla Campbell

So Sweet

Collaging techniques make this trio of gift tags, *left,* work especially well. Erin Terrell incorporated flowers, bold eyelets, ribbons, and other embellishments for shape and texture. To soften the edges of the tags, she rubbed them with sandpaper or an ink pad.

Designs by Erin Terrell

A PETITE PACKAGE

A tag wrapped to look like a tiny gift offers a little something extra to the lucky recipient. This whimsical tag by Susan Badgett can be customized to match any wrapped present. Decorate the "package" as you like, and add a ribbon bow to the top for a realistic touch. Patterns begin on page 92.

Design by Susan Badgett

Two-Tone Tag

Experimenting with a mix of complementary paper patterns adds richness to cards and tags, as Alison Beachem demonstrates with this Mother's Day gift tag, *above*. Alison selected a stripe that coordinates with the florals, using the stripes as the dominant pattern and merely accenting with the others.

Design by Alison Beachem

Holiday Lights

Crimped silver paper gives this holiday lightbulb by Jodi Sanford, *below*, an authentic metallic look. The curled wire is secured between the layers. Jodi attached the layered name tag with a small brad. Patterns begin on page 92.

Design by Jodi Sanford

Understated Elegance

A simple gift tag by Charla Campbell, *above*, clearly identifies the recipients. She matted the tag sections to add a touch of class, and for dimension, she crinkled and chalked the punched flowers gracing the bottom corners.

Design by Charla Campbell

FLY AWAY

A button-winged ladybug tag is an appropriate topper for a gift you bring to an outdoor party. Polly McMillan layered red card stock and blue plaid paper on beige card stock and then topped it all with a die-cut ladybug. To embellish the die cut, she threaded buttons on top of two of the bug's spots. A message and long dashed border lines drawn in black ink complete the tag.

Design by Polly McMillan

Snowflake Surprise

Off-kilter placement of three-dimensional elements makes this tag by Jodi Sanford, *left,* stand out in the crowd. Jodi made the tag by attaching a small rectangle of patterned paper to a piece of white card stock and using strips of card stock for the title. The recipient's name is printed on clear film, and a snowflake eyelet secures a piece of mesh. She finished by wrapping fibers around the tag and setting a small brad at the top.

Design by Jodi Sanford

Seasonal Charm

To celebrate an autumn event, Charla Campbell topped her gift with the seasonal tag, *above.* The rust card stock tag is divided into six pencil-marked sections, each framing a tiny centered leaf charm. Charla covered the front of the tag with sheer fabric and taped it on the back. To emphasize the six sections, she hand-stitched along the pencil lines with tan embroidery floss. The tag is finished with a card stock backing, a brass mini brad, and strands of gold floss looped around the brad prongs and then inserted into the hole.

Design by Charla Campbell

Pinned Together

An embossing template makes these gift tags, *above,* a snap to put together. Kathleen Paneitz printed the message on white card stock and then added a layer of patterned vellum in the appropriate color. She embossed the diaper pin on white card stock and cut the pin head from colored card stock. After embossing, she sprinkled glitter on the head. A punched hole is threaded with cording to hang the tag.

Designs by Kathleen Paneitz

Pattern *Section*

Our patterns are provided for the personal use of our readers.
Resize as needed to fit your layouts.

10, 9, 8 ... , page 61

Champagne

Champagne
Flute

Invitation
Front

Offer a Toast, page 61

Winter Warmth, *page 22*

The Bunny Hop, *page 25*

Tree Top

Tree
Trunk

Pretty in Pastels, *page 85*

Halloween

Visit Our "Web Site," *page 72*

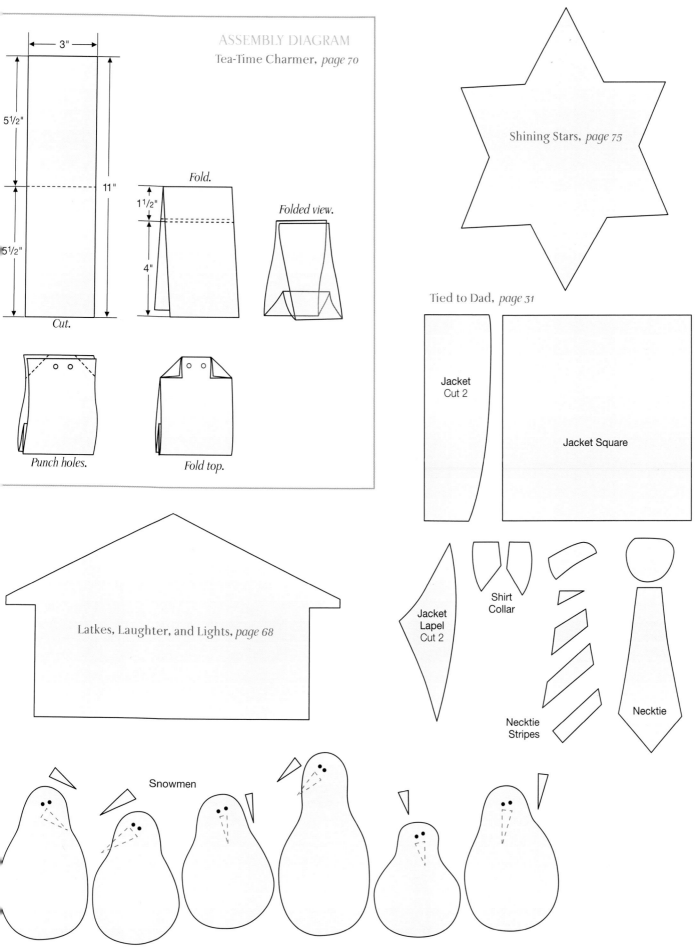

ASSEMBLY DIAGRAM
Tea-Time Charmer, *page 70*

3"

5½"

11"

5½"

Cut.

Fold.

1½"

4"

Folded view.

Punch holes.

Fold top.

Shining Stars, *page 75*

Tied to Dad, *page 31*

Jacket
Cut 2

Jacket Square

Jacket
Lapel
Cut 2

Shirt
Collar

Necktie
Stripes

Necktie

Latkes, Laughter, and Lights, *page 68*

Snowmen

A Trio of Well-Wishers, *page 20* and Snowman Line-up, *page 21*

Ghostly Notes, *page 33*

Quilling steps for The Sky's the Limit, *page 11*, and Graceful Swirls and Whirls, *page 41*.

Step 1   Step 2   Step 3

Graceful Swirls and Whirls, *page 41*

The Sky's the Limit, *page 11*

cut out cut out cut out punch out

Slider Statement, *page 7*

Holiday Lights, *page 89*

Sharing Patriotism, *page 29*

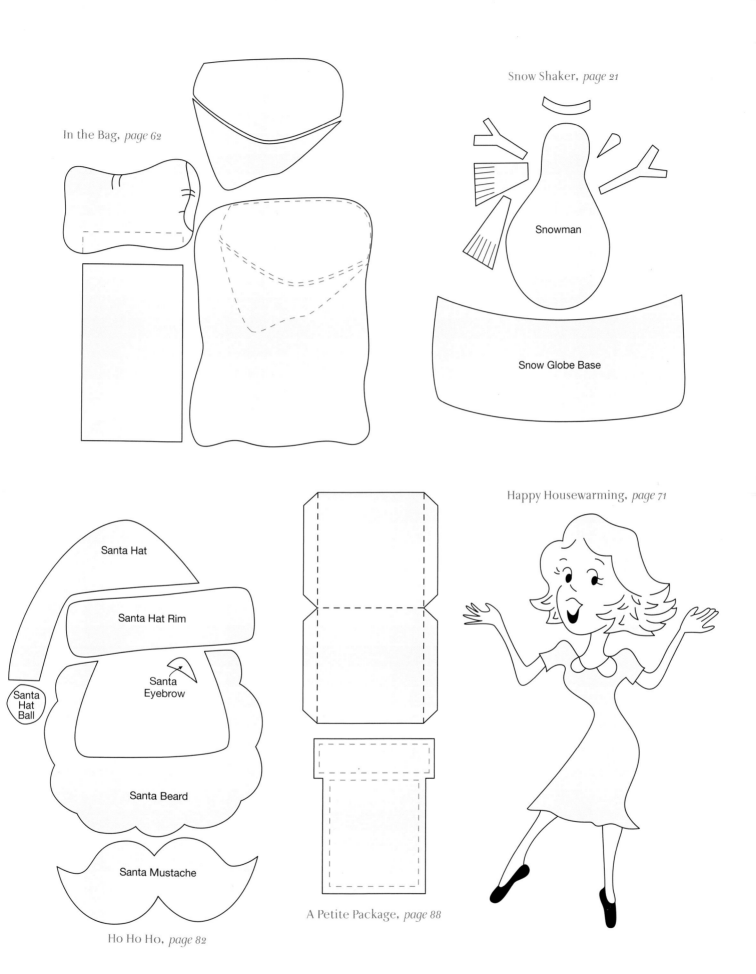

In the Bag, *page 62*

Snow Shaker, *page 21*

Snowman

Snow Globe Base

Happy Housewarming, *page 71*

Santa Hat

Santa Hat Rim

Santa Eyebrow

Santa Hat Ball

Santa Beard

Santa Mustache

Ho Ho Ho, *page 82*

A Petite Package, *page 88*

Better Homes and Gardens®
Creative Collection™

Editorial Director
Gayle Goodson Butler

Editor-in-Chief
Beverly Rivers

Executive Editor   Karman Wittry Hotchkiss
Contributing Editorial Manager   Heidi Palkovic
Contributing Design Director   Tracy DeVenney

Contributing Editor   Kathy Roth Eastman
Contributing Graphic Designer   Jodi Mensing
Copy Chief   Mary Heaton
Contributing Copy Editor   Dave Kirchner
Contributing Proofreader   Joleen Ross
Administrative Assistant   Lori Eggers

Executive Vice President
Bob Mate

Publishing Group President
Jack Griffin

Chairman and CEO   William T. Kerr
President and COO   Stephen M. Lacy

In Memoriam
E. T. Meredith III (1933–2003)